The Best Salesman in the World!

Evelyn Wright

Evelyn Wright

Copyright Page

Index

Evelyn Wright

Customer Psychology

Customer psychology is at the heart of any successful sale. At its core, selling is not just about offering a product or service, but about understanding what really drives people to buy. Customers don't buy just because they need something, but because they feel an emotional connection or because they perceive a value that goes beyond the tangible. A good salesperson must understand these emotions and motivations in order to create a shopping experience that resonates deeply with the customer.

It all starts with empathy. A salesperson must put themselves in the customer's shoes and understand their situation, their problems, and their desires. It's not about pushing the product that will bring the most profit to the company, but about offering what the customer really needs. For example, if someone comes into a store looking for a solution to sleep better, the salesperson should not simply offer them the most expensive pillow. They should ask questions, listen, and find out if the problem is really the pillow, or if there are other factors, such as stress, that are affecting their rest. By understanding the root of the problem, the salesperson can offer a more accurate and relevant solution, which makes the customer feel that they have been heard and that the purchase was their own decision, not something forced on them.

A fundamental aspect of customer psychology is the perception of value. People don't always look for the cheapest product, but rather the one that offers them the most value. This value can be tangible, such as the durability of a product, or intangible, such as the emotional satisfaction that comes from having something that is unique or that improves their quality of life. Customers want to feel that they are making a smart choice, and part of being a good salesperson is knowing how to communicate that value clearly and attractively. For example, a car is not just a means of transportation; it can be a style statement, a symbol of success, or a guarantee of security for the family. The salesperson must connect the product with the customer's personal values.

Psychology also tells us that customers want to feel like they are in control. No one likes to feel like they are being pressured into buying something. A successful salesperson should avoid pushy tactics and instead guide the customer to discover the benefits of the product or service for themselves. This is accomplished by asking open-ended questions, giving the customer room to reflect, and providing helpful information without overwhelming them. For example, instead of saying "you should buy this because it is the best," a good salesperson might say "how would you feel if this could solve that problem?" In this way, the customer feels empowered to make their own decision.

Another key point is the fear of loss, one of the most powerful emotions in the buying process. People fear missing out on an opportunity, and sellers can use this concept to motivate action without making the customer feel like they are being manipulated. This doesn't mean pushing with phrases like "buy now or miss out," but rather creating a genuine sense of urgency by highlighting the opportunity to improve the customer's life if they act in time. A simple example is mentioning that certain benefits or special prices will be available for a limited time only, but always from a transparent and sincere approach.

Trust is another essential psychological factor in any sales process. Customers need to feel like they are dealing with someone who is authentic and has their best interest in mind. To build trust, a salesperson must be honest, deliver on their promises, and demonstrate knowledge. It is important not to inflate the benefits of a product or service beyond what it can offer, because that creates unrealistic expectations that can lead to disappointment. When a salesperson is transparent and admits the limitations of what they sell, customers tend to appreciate them more and trust that the recommendations are genuine.

Finally, repetition and recognition also play a crucial role. Familiarity breeds trust, and that's why customers tend to buy brands or products they've seen or heard of several times. A good salesperson should remember this and not get discouraged if a customer doesn't buy right away. Sometimes, they simply need time to process the information, compare options, and come back with a greater willingness to close the purchase. Patience and gentle persistence, without overwhelming the customer, are key to tapping into this part of customer psychology.

In short, customer psychology is the art of understanding what motivates people to buy and how a salesperson can positively influence that decision without being pushy or manipulative. It's about creating empathy, conveying value, giving the customer control, and building a relationship based on trust. A good salesperson is one who knows how to listen, understands their customer's emotions, and creates a shopping experience in which the customer feels valued and satisfied.

Connecting with the Client

Connecting with the customer is one of the most important pillars of any sale. To get someone to buy, you first have to create a genuine relationship, a connection that goes beyond simply exchanging money for a product or service. This type of connection is based on trust, empathy, and above all, the ability to make the customer feel understood and valued. In this chapter, we will look at how a good salesperson can build these relationships authentically and how that connection is what really drives sales in the long run.

Imagine walking into a store and the salesperson immediately approaches you with a list of deals or promotions. You may not be ready to make a purchasing decision at the time. But if that salesperson takes the time to greet you, make you feel welcome, and ask how they can help you, the situation changes. You feel less like a number and more like a person. That's the difference between a cold sale and a sale that's built on a connection. A good salesperson knows that before they sell, they must listen.

Listening is key. Many salespeople make the mistake of talking too much, trying to impress the customer with technical features or statistics that they don't really care about. But when a salesperson listens, they can find out exactly what the customer needs, their concerns, and their desires. For example, if a person walks into a store looking for a sofa, a salesperson who only focuses on the quality of the material or discounts may lose the sale. In contrast, a salesperson who asks, "What kind of sofa are you looking for?" or "What is the space like where you plan to put it?" opens the door for a deeper conversation. As the customer responds, the salesperson can tailor their offer to those specific needs, showing that they are genuinely interested in helping, not just selling.

In addition to listening, another fundamental aspect of connecting with the customer is empathy. Empathy is the ability to put yourself in another person's shoes, to understand what they feel or what they are looking for. A customer does not always buy a product because they urgently need it; sometimes there is an emotional reason behind that purchase. A good salesperson knows how to recognize those emotions and use that knowledge to create a more personalized experience.

For example, if a customer is looking for a bicycle for their child, an empathetic salesperson will not only talk about the type of wheels or the frame material, but will also discuss how that bicycle can become the perfect gift that will bring moments of happiness and adventure to their child. In this way, the salesperson is not only selling a product, but an experience and an emotion.

Trust is another essential component. Trust is not built overnight, but it can be lost in a second if the customer feels like they are being tricked or manipulated. A good salesperson is always honest and transparent. They don't try to hide information or exaggerate the benefits of a product just to close a sale. If something has a limitation or isn't suitable for the customer, they say so clearly. This honesty creates a sense of security in the customer, who will know that they are dealing with someone who cares more about their well-being than earning a quick commission. In fact, many customers will return to a salesperson who was honest, even if they didn't buy anything the first time.

In addition to honesty, another important element in building a connection is personal treatment. Remembering customers' names, preferences, or even small details about their lives can make a big difference. Customers want to feel special, not like they're just another transaction in the day. A salesperson who greets a customer by name or remembers that the last time they came in they were looking for something specific shows that they really pay attention. This level of personalization is what makes customers feel valued and increases the chances that they'll return.

An additional aspect that is often overlooked is the importance of patience. Some customers need time to make decisions, and that is where a good salesperson knows how to give space without losing the connection. An impatient salesperson who pressures the customer to buy can lead to rejection. On the other hand, a salesperson who shows understanding, who gives time to think and offers help at any time, generates a feeling of trust and security. Sometimes, customers come back weeks or months later, not because the salesperson pursued them, but because they gave them the time they needed and, in that process, built a relationship of respect.

It's also important to consider body language. Often, what we say with our bodies is more powerful than words. A salesperson who makes eye contact, smiles, and has an open posture conveys warmth and approachability. On the other hand, crossing their arms, looking at their watch, or looking distracted sends negative signals, even if the words are correct. A good salesperson is aware of these small details and makes sure their body language is aligned with the message they want to convey: "I'm here to help you, not pressure you."

Connecting with the customer is ultimately a process that requires time, dedication and authenticity. It is not about quick tricks or techniques to manipulate people, but about building a relationship based on trust and mutual respect. A customer who feels that they have been understood and valued will not only buy more readily, but will also recommend the seller to others, creating a network of connections that can lead to exponential sales in the long run.

In short, a good salesperson is not just someone who knows how to close a sale. It is someone who knows how to open a conversation, how to listen, how to be empathetic, and most importantly, how to make the customer feel like they are a unique and valuable person in the entire buying process. Connecting with the customer is the foundation on which all successful sales are built.

The Art of Active Listening

The art of active listening is one of the most powerful skills a salesperson can master. On the surface, listening seems like something we all know how to do. However, active listening is very different from simply hearing. It's about paying full attention, understanding what the other person is saying and sometimes what they're not saying. A salesperson who actively listens is able to pick up on the customer's true needs, concerns, and desires, allowing them to offer the perfect solution instead of just trying to sell the first thing that comes to mind.

Active listening starts with a willingness to be present in the conversation. This means turning off any distractions, both mental and physical. When a customer is talking, it's easy for a salesperson to get distracted by other thoughts, such as thinking about the next sale, what to say next, or even how much time is left until closing for the day. But a salesperson who is truly customer-focused puts all of that aside and concentrates on every word the person is saying. That level of attention not only allows you to better understand the customer, but it also sends the message that their opinions matter.

A key aspect of active listening is asking open-ended questions. Instead of asking questions that can only be answered with a "yes" or "no," a good salesperson should ask questions that invite the customer to talk more and share details about what they really need. For example, instead of asking, "Are you looking for a computer?" an open-ended question would be, "What types of activities do you plan to use the computer for?" These types of questions not only provide more useful information for the salesperson, but they also make the customer feel heard and valued. By asking open-ended questions, the salesperson demonstrates a genuine interest in the customer's needs, which strengthens the relationship between the two.

Another key technique within the art of active listening is feedback. This means repeating or paraphrasing what the customer has said to make sure you have understood them correctly. For example, if a customer mentions that they are looking for a quick solution to a specific problem, the salesperson can respond, "So, if I understand correctly, the most important thing for you is to find a solution that saves you time, correct?" By doing this, you not only ensure that you are both on the same page, but you also show that you are really paying attention. Furthermore, this technique helps the customer clarify their own thoughts and dig deeper into what they are really looking for.

Active listening also involves being aware of the customer's emotions, not just their words. Sometimes, the customer may say one thing, but their tone of voice or body language indicates something else. A good salesperson knows how to read these cues and adjust their approach. For example, if a customer seems hesitant or worried, instead of rushing to close the sale, the salesperson can pause and ask something like, "Is there anything that concerns you about this option?" Not only does this question show empathy, it can also reveal doubts or concerns that the customer may not have expressed directly.

Additionally, silence is a powerful tool in the process of active listening. Often, salespeople feel the need to fill in every blank space with words, but sometimes it's better to just stay silent for a moment and let the customer reflect. Silence gives the customer the time needed to think and formulate their responses without feeling like they're being rushed. It also allows the salesperson to pick up on any additional information that may emerge when the customer takes that time to reflect. Many times, in those moments of pause, customers reveal key information that can be crucial to understanding what they really want.

Active listening not only helps the salesperson better understand the customer's needs, but it also builds trust. Customers value a salesperson who listens to them because it shows respect and consideration. They feel understood, which creates an emotional connection that goes beyond the simple business transaction. In a world where people often feel ignored or unheard, a salesperson who really pays attention can stand out and create a lasting relationship with the customer. Not only does this generate sales in the present, but it also increases the chances that the customer will return in the future or recommend the service to others.

A common mistake many salespeople make is interrupting the customer while they are speaking. Sometimes, the salesperson thinks they have already understood what the customer needs and rushes to offer a solution. But by doing so, they risk missing important details or making the customer feel slighted. Active listening involves letting the customer finish speaking before responding. Even if the salesperson already has the answer, they should give the customer space to fully express their thoughts and concerns. This patience not only improves communication, but it also reinforces the idea that the salesperson is there to help, not just sell.

Finally, the art of active listening is something that is honed with practice. It's not a skill that is mastered overnight, but the more a salesperson tries it, the more natural it will become. Over time, you'll learn to better read customers' verbal and nonverbal cues, ask the right questions, and create an environment where the customer feels comfortable sharing information. By doing so, you'll not only be more effective at closing sales, but you'll also improve your ability to create lasting relationships with customers.

In conclusion, active listening is an essential skill for any salesperson who wants to be successful in the long run. It involves giving the customer full attention, asking open-ended questions, offering feedback, and being aware of both words and emotions. By mastering this art, a salesperson will not only sell more, but will also build a solid foundation of trust and loyalty with their customers, which will be key to continued success.

Ethical Persuasion Techniques

Ethical persuasion techniques are an essential part of a good salesperson's job. Persuasion is not the same as manipulation. While manipulation seeks to control or force someone to do something against their will, ethical persuasion is based on influencing in an honest and respectful way, helping the customer make decisions that are beneficial to them. A salesperson who uses ethical persuasion is not simply looking to make a quick sale, but to build a relationship of trust and ensure that the customer truly sees the value in what they are buying.

The first principle of ethical persuasion is sincerity. A salesperson must be honest at all times, and this includes being clear about the benefits and limitations of their product or service. If a customer feels like they are being misled, they will lose trust, not only in the salesperson, but in the brand or company they represent. Sincerity is the foundation of a trusting relationship, and when a customer trusts the salesperson, they are much more likely to feel comfortable making purchasing decisions. Ethical persuasion requires the salesperson to be transparent, not exaggerating or promising things they cannot deliver. If a product has a downside, it is best to mention it openly so the customer can make an informed decision.

Another important element of ethical persuasion is the focus on benefits, not just features. Sometimes salespeople focus too much on describing the technical details of a product or highlighting superficial features, but what really convinces the customer is how that product will improve their life. For example, if someone is looking for a vacuum cleaner, the salesperson might start by talking about the power of the motor or the suction capacity. However, the most persuasive thing would be to talk about how that vacuum cleaner will allow them to clean faster, with less effort, and enjoy a cleaner home in less time. Instead of overwhelming the customer with technical data, the salesperson should focus on how the product or service will meet the customer's needs and wants in a real, tangible way.

Empathy also plays a key role in ethical persuasion. A salesperson must be able to put themselves in the customer's shoes and understand their concerns, doubts, and expectations. Empathy allows the salesperson to adjust their approach to make it more relevant and personal. For example, if a customer is concerned about the price of a product, an empathetic salesperson won't simply try to convince them to buy something expensive without further ado. Instead, they might show alternatives within the customer's budget or explain how the investment in that specific product is justified in the long run by durability or future savings. In this way, the customer feels that their concerns are being heard and taken into account, which builds trust and opens the door to more ethical and authentic selling.

A very effective ethical persuasion technique is the creation of scarcity or urgency, but it must be used carefully and honestly. The idea behind scarcity is that when something is limited, it becomes more valuable in the eyes of the customer. A salesperson may mention that a product has a limited number of units or that a special offer is available for a limited time only. However, it is crucial that this information is real and not a tactic to pressure the customer dishonestly. If a customer feels that they are being tricked with false offers or with products that are not actually that limited, the effect will be counterproductive. Scarcity should be an ethical tool, not a way to manipulate.

Another ethical persuasion technique is the use of social proof. People like to know that others have had good experiences with a product or service before they make a decision. A seller can share testimonials from satisfied customers, positive reviews, or case studies that show how other people in similar situations have found value in the product. Not only does this reassure the customer, but it also reinforces the idea that the product has already proven its worth. However, it is important that this social proof is genuine and not fabricated. In the digital age, customers can easily spot when a review is fake or exaggerated, and that can seriously damage the seller's credibility.

The principle of reciprocity is another ethical persuasion technique. Reciprocity is based on the idea that when someone gives us something, we feel a desire to return the favor. In the context of sales, a salesperson may offer something valuable to the customer before asking them to buy. This can be helpful information, a small sample of the product, or heartfelt advice. By offering something first, the salesperson creates a feeling of gratitude in the customer, making it more likely that the customer will be willing to buy. The key here, however, is that what is offered must have value to the customer and should not seem like it is designed solely to force them to buy. Reciprocity works best when the customer feels like they are receiving something that really matters to them, not just a superficial gift.

Commitment and consistency are also important in ethical persuasion. People tend to want to be consistent with their previous decisions. If a customer has already shown interest in a product or made a small decision, they are more likely to follow through with a larger purchase. An ethical salesperson can take advantage of this by asking the customer to commit to something small first. For example, if a customer is interested in a free trial service or an initial consultation, they are more likely to follow through with a larger purchase later. The important thing is that the salesperson does not force the customer to make commitments they do not want or need, but rather naturally guides them toward decisions that are consistent with their wants and needs.

Finally, one of the most effective ethical persuasion techniques is building a long-term relationship. A good salesperson isn't interested only in closing a sale today; they are also focused on building a long-lasting relationship with the customer. This means that the salesperson must be willing to continue helping and providing value even after the sale has closed. Customers value salespeople who care about their long-term satisfaction, not just the moment of purchase. By building relationships based on trust and respect, a salesperson can secure repeat sales and word-of-mouth referrals, which are some of the most valuable ways to grow in the world of sales.

In short, ethical persuasion techniques are not about manipulating or forcing the customer to buy something. They are about understanding the customer's needs, being honest, building trust, and offering real value. By using techniques such as empathy, reciprocity, social proof, and engagement, a salesperson can persuade in an ethical manner, creating a positive buying experience for both the customer and themselves. This approach not only generates short-term sales, but also builds long-term relationships based on mutual respect and customer satisfaction.

Evelyn Wright

The Power of Effective Presentation

The power of an effective presentation is one of the most valuable tools in a good salesperson's arsenal. A well-made presentation can be the difference between closing a sale and losing the opportunity. But it's not just about superficially showing a product or service. The key is how you communicate the value of what you offer, how you capture the customer's attention and maintain their interest throughout the entire process. A salesperson who knows how to make an effective presentation manages to connect with their audience and, most importantly, generate trust and enthusiasm.

The first thing to understand about an effective presentation is that it must be customer-centric. Many salespeople make the mistake of focusing only on the product, describing its technical features or talking endlessly about how wonderful it is. However, what really matters to the customer is not the product itself, but how that product can improve their life or solve a specific problem. That's why the focus should always be on the benefits, not the features. The customer wants to know how what is being presented to them is going to make their life easier, more comfortable, or more satisfying. An effective presentation answers those questions right from the start.

To achieve this customer-centric approach, the salesperson must prepare their presentation in advance, researching who their audience is and what their needs are. No two customers are the same, so a presentation that works perfectly for one may not be effective for another. Personalization is key. Before presenting, the salesperson should have asked questions, listened carefully, and gathered the information necessary to tailor their message to the customer's specific concerns and desires. This shows that the salesperson is not just interested in making a quick sale, but in offering a real solution that provides value.

Another crucial aspect of effective presentation is clarity. Simplicity in communication is powerful. A common mistake is to try to impress the client with technical language or complicated explanations that end up confusing more than clarifying. A good salesperson knows that their goal is not to demonstrate how much they know, but to make the client clearly understand the value of what they are offering. To do that, it is essential to use simple language, avoid unnecessary jargon, and structure the presentation in a way that is easy to follow. The message must be clear from the beginning: what is being offered, why it is important to the client, and how it will solve their problems.

Using stories is one of the most effective techniques for making a presentation memorable. People love to hear stories because they are easy to understand and remember. A salesperson can take advantage of this by telling a story that illustrates how their product or service has helped other people in similar situations. Stories make the customer connect emotionally with the presentation, because they are not just receiving data, but a tangible experience that they can imagine in their own life. For example, instead of simply saying that a software will increase productivity, you could tell the story of how a company similar to the customer's increased their efficiency by 30% using that same software. This allows the customer to visualize the success in their own context.

Body language also plays a big role in effective presentation. It's not just about what you say, but how you say it. A salesperson who is enthusiastic about what they are presenting conveys that enthusiasm to the customer. If the salesperson seems bored or uninterested, the customer will be too. That's why it's critical to maintain an open posture, make eye contact, and use gestures that reinforce the message. A genuine smile, an energetic tone of voice, and a positive attitude can make the customer feel more comfortable and receptive. In addition, the customer's body language is also important. A good salesperson should be aware of the signals the customer is sending, whether it's interest, doubt, or confusion, so they can adjust their approach in real time.

Customer interaction is essential during the presentation. A common mistake is to turn the presentation into a monologue, where the salesperson talks without pause while the customer just passively listens. An effective presentation is a conversation. The salesperson should ask questions during the presentation, not only to keep the customer engaged, but also to ensure that he or she is addressing his or her specific concerns. Questions like "Does this answer what you were looking for?" or "Do you find this solution useful for your situation?" invite the customer to actively participate in the conversation and give the salesperson the opportunity to adjust his or her presentation as needed.

The hands-on demonstration is another powerful tool in an effective presentation. When possible, allowing the customer to see the product in action or experience it firsthand can be much more persuasive than any verbal description. If a salesperson is presenting software, for example, it would be helpful to do a live demonstration so the customer can see how easy it is to use and the results it can generate. If a physical product is being sold, allowing the customer to touch it, try it out, or experience it in some concrete way can create a much stronger emotional connection than simply describing it. Hands-on demonstrations give the customer the chance to see with their own eyes what the salesperson is talking about.

Objection handling is an essential component of any effective presentation.

Throughout the presentation, the customer is likely to have questions or concerns. A good salesperson should not ignore these objections or treat them as an obstacle. Instead, they should view them as an opportunity to clear up misunderstandings, provide more information, and build customer confidence. When a customer raises an objection, the salesperson should listen attentively, validate the customer's concern, and then offer a reassuring response. For example, if a customer is concerned about price, the salesperson can explain how the long-term value of the product justifies the initial investment. Handling objections calmly and respectfully shows that the salesperson is committed to helping the customer make the best decision possible.

Closing the presentation is a crucial moment. After all the benefits have been presented and the value of the product or service demonstrated, the salesperson should make a clear call to action. This doesn't mean pressuring the customer into making a hasty decision, but rather gently guiding them to the next step. It can be as simple as asking, "Would you like us to get started on this?" or "What's the next step you'd like to take?" The closing should be natural and based on everything that has been previously discussed. A good salesperson knows that an effective presentation is not only informative, but it also inspires confidence in the customer to move forward with the purchase.

In conclusion, the power of an effective presentation lies in its ability to communicate value in a clear, personal and compelling way. A salesperson who focuses on the customer's needs, who uses stories, who actively interacts and who skillfully handles objections is much more prepared to successfully close a sale. The presentation is not just an opportunity to showcase a product or service, but to create a genuine connection with the customer and demonstrate that what is being offered is the best solution for them.

Creating Urgency Without Pressure

Creating urgency without pressuring the customer is one of the most delicate, but also most effective, strategies a salesperson can master. Urgency, when used well, can motivate the customer to make a quick decision, but when handled poorly, it can feel like pressure and cause rejection. It is a balance that a good salesperson must learn to master, always respecting the customer's pace and avoiding making them feel obligated or forced to buy.

Urgency is all about conveying to the customer that there is a legitimate reason to act now rather than later. The human brain tends to avoid difficult decisions or put them off if it doesn't feel a compelling reason to make them at the moment. So creating a sense of urgency can help the customer focus on what's at stake and understand that acting now is better than waiting. The trick, however, is to do so without seeming desperate or manipulative. The customer should feel that the decision to act soon is logical and beneficial, not something imposed by the salesperson.

A first step to effectively creating urgency is to present legitimate, real reasons why it's worth buying now. This can be something as simple as a promotion that's about to expire, limited stock, or an exclusive, limited-time offer. The key is that these reasons need to be authentic. Many customers are already aware of common sales tactics used to create a false sense of urgency, and if they sense that something isn't genuine, they'll lose trust in the salesperson and likely not buy. For example, if a salesperson continually repeats that "there are only a few units left" or "the offer ends today" and that's not true, the customer will quickly notice. Trust is key, and any urgency strategy needs to be based on real facts.

Another way to create urgency without being pressurizing is to highlight the immediate benefits the customer will gain by taking action now. Instead of focusing solely on the fact that the product is on sale for a limited time, a good salesperson will talk about how the customer can start enjoying those benefits right away. For example, if a customer is interested in a personal improvement service, the salesperson might say something like, "If we get started now, you could start seeing results in just a few weeks." This approach focuses on the value the customer will gain the sooner they make the decision. Instead of feeling pressured, the customer will feel that acting now will allow them to improve their situation faster.

Using social proof can also be a great way to create urgency without seeming manipulative. Humans tend to act when they see others making similar decisions. If the customer knows that many other people are making the same decision and benefiting from it, they are more likely to want to act as well. For example, a salesperson might mention that other customers have already taken advantage of the current offer and are seeing great results. This technique works because the customer feels like they are missing out on an opportunity that others have already taken advantage of. However, it is important that the social proof used is true and not made up just to pressure the customer.

Additionally, real scarcity is a powerful way to create urgency. People value things that are limited or hard to get more. When a product is in limited supply or a special offer is only available to a small number of people, the customer will feel they need to act soon to avoid missing out on the opportunity. Again, the key is that this scarcity must be genuine. If a seller promises that a product is about to go out of stock and then the customer finds out that it is still available weeks later, credibility is destroyed. Honesty is always key in any urgency strategy.

A good salesperson also knows to let the customer feel in control of the situation. Even if the salesperson presents clear reasons for acting soon, the customer should feel free to make the decision in his or her own time. This means that even if you present facts that create urgency, you should not push the customer with questions like, "So do you buy it now or do you let it go?" Instead, a better strategy would be to ask open-ended questions that invite the customer to reflect on what they would lose if they don't take action soon, such as, "Would you like to start enjoying these benefits now or would you rather wait?" This keeps the urgency in the customer's mind, but in a subtle and respectful way, giving them space to think without feeling pressured.

Transparency is also crucial to ethically creating urgency. A salesperson who is clear about the reasons why a deal is limited or why it is important to act soon builds trust. For example, if a discount is only available until a specific date, it is helpful for the salesperson to explain why that deal exists and when exactly it ends. A salesperson can say something like, "This special deal is available because we are celebrating our anniversary, and it ends on Friday." This provides context that makes sense to the customer and gives them a legitimate reason to consider acting now, without making them feel pressured.

Another technique that can help create urgency without pressure is focusing on the costs of not taking action. Sometimes, customers need to be made aware of what they will lose if they don't act now. However, this strategy should be used carefully and always with a positive approach. Instead of scaring the customer or making them feel bad about not buying, the salesperson can gently highlight the benefits they are missing out on by not taking action. For example, a salesperson might say, "I know it's an investment, but think about how much you could save in the long run if you start now instead of waiting." This gets the customer thinking about the future value without feeling pressured or obligated.

Personalization also plays a big role in creating urgency. Not all customers respond the same way to urgency, so it's essential for the salesperson to tailor their approach based on each customer's personality and needs. Some customers may need a more direct nudge, while others prefer a more subtle approach. An experienced salesperson knows when the right time is to mention urgency and how to do it in a way that the customer appreciates and sees it as a positive.

Finally, it's important to remember that urgency isn't always about discounts or promotions. Sometimes urgency can be created by showing the customer how they can improve their life right away. For example, a salesperson might say, "The sooner you start using this product, the faster you'll start seeing results." This creates a sense of urgency based on value, not the need to take advantage of a temporary offer. When the customer sees that acting now will allow them to improve their situation sooner, they're more likely to make a quick decision without feeling pressured.

In short, creating urgency without pressure is a skill that requires balance and tact. The salesperson must provide genuine reasons for the customer to act soon, but always in an honest and respectful manner. By focusing on immediate benefits, using social proof, offering real scarcity, and allowing the customer to maintain control, it is possible to create a sense of urgency that motivates without creating discomfort. Well-managed urgency can be a powerful tool that not only drives sales, but also creates a positive customer experience.

Automation and Smart Sales with AI

Automation and smart selling with artificial intelligence (AI) are revolutionizing the world of sales. A few years ago, many of the tasks that can now be performed automatically required the direct effort of salespeople, which meant more time and energy invested in repetitive tasks. Today, thanks to technology, especially AI, it is possible to simplify many of these processes, making them more efficient and accurate. This not only allows salespeople to focus on what really matters, such as building relationships and closing sales, but also gives them a competitive advantage in an increasingly fast-paced market.

Automation in sales involves using technological tools to perform tasks that would normally require human intervention, but in a faster and more efficient way. For example, you can automate sending personalized emails to potential customers, managing inventory, following up with clients, or even segmenting audiences. All of this reduces the time a salesperson has to spend on administrative tasks and increases productivity. However, what's really interesting is how artificial intelligence takes automation to a whole new level, making sales not only faster, but smarter too.

AI has the ability to analyze large amounts of data in a matter of seconds and detect patterns that humans might miss. This capability is key to smart selling because it allows salespeople to better understand their customers and predict their needs before they even identify them. For example, AI tools can analyze customers' purchasing behavior, interaction history, and demographic profile to suggest specific products or services that are most likely to interest them. This type of personalized selling, powered by AI, significantly increases the chances of closing a sale because it is based on real data and not assumptions.

One of the ways AI can improve customer experience is through the automatic personalization of interactions. Previously, salespeople had to research and remember details about each customer manually. Now, AI can do this in real-time, providing salespeople with the information they need instantly. For example, if a customer has shown interest in certain products in the past, AI can suggest personalized recommendations at the right time, based on their previous preferences. This makes the customer feel valued and understood, which in turn creates a stronger connection with the salesperson and the brand. Additionally, by automating these processes, salespeople can focus on more complex tasks, such as developing closing strategies and addressing more detailed queries.

Another key benefit of AI in sales is its ability to predict customer behavior. AI tools can analyze historical data and behavioral patterns to anticipate when a customer is ready to make a purchase. This allows salespeople to intervene at just the right time, offering the right product or service at the instant when the customer is most receptive. Instead of waiting for the customer to take the initiative, AI can send an alert to the salesperson to contact that customer or even automatically generate a special offer that incentivizes them to take action. This predictive capability not only speeds up the sales process, but also increases the likelihood of success.

Additionally, AI can also help in the prospecting phase. Instead of salespeople spending hours searching for new leads or trying to determine who might be interested in their product, AI can analyze huge databases and detect which people or companies are most likely to become customers. This is done by analyzing a variety of factors, such as purchase history, social media interactions, or even online mentions of keywords related to the product or service. In this way, AI can generate a list of qualified leads, allowing salespeople to focus their efforts on contacts who are most likely to close a sale, rather than wasting time on cold prospects.

The use of chatbots is another clear example of how AI is changing sales. Chatbots can interact with customers in real-time, answering common questions, helping to select products, or guiding the customer through the purchasing process. Best of all, these chatbots are available 24/7, meaning customers can get assistance at any time, even outside of business hours. While chatbots don't completely replace a human salesperson, they can handle simple, repetitive tasks, allowing the sales team to focus on more complex situations that require a personal touch. Plus, many chatbots are designed to learn from each interaction, meaning they get smarter and more efficient over time.

AI-powered data analytics tools also play a crucial role in improving sales strategies. A salesperson working with AI can access detailed reports that show which strategies are working and which are not. For example, AI can analyze what type of marketing messages generate the most sales, which communication channels are most effective, and which products have the best response across different customer groups. This information is invaluable because it allows sales strategies to be adjusted in real time, optimizing each step of the process for better results. Instead of relying on intuition or lengthy testing, AI provides clear, concrete data that guides the sales team's decisions.

AI can also be used to automate the follow-up process. Following up is a critical part of sales, but it is often one of the most time-consuming tasks. With the help of AI, salespeople can schedule automatic reminders to send follow-up emails or messages at key times. Additionally, AI can analyze customer responses to these follow-ups and adjust the approach based on how they react. For example, if a customer opens multiple emails but doesn't make a purchase, AI can suggest sending a personalized offer or making a follow-up call instead of continuing with the same approach. This ensures that the follow-up is relevant and effective, rather than coming across as spammy.

Another important aspect of AI is its ability to improve the customer experience through sentiment analysis. Some AI tools can analyze the tone of voice or language used in emails, calls, or text messages to determine whether a customer is satisfied, frustrated, or hesitant. This information is invaluable to salespeople, as it allows them to adjust their approach in real time. If a customer appears frustrated, the salesperson can step in to resolve the issue before it becomes a bigger roadblock to the sale. On the other hand, if a customer shows signs of excitement, the salesperson can use that moment to close the sale. This ability to read customer emotions digitally is something that only AI can deliver on a large scale.

It's important to note that while automation and AI can do a lot to improve the sales process, they don't completely replace the human touch. Sales is still, at its core, a human-to-human interaction. Customers value empathy, trust, and the relationship they build with the salesperson. AI and automation are powerful tools that can help salespeople be more effective, but sales success still depends on the salesperson's ability to genuinely connect with their customers. The key is to use these tools to free up time and energy, allowing the salesperson to focus on interactions that require a human touch and building long-term relationships with customers.

In short, automation and AI-powered smart selling are transforming the way business is done. These technologies not only enable salespeople to be more efficient, but also improve the accuracy and personalization of customer interactions. By using AI to analyze data, predict behavior, and automate repetitive tasks, salespeople can focus on what really matters: delivering solutions that add value to their customers' lives. In the future, salespeople who make the most of these technological tools will have a clear advantage over the competition, not only by selling more, but by doing so in a smarter and more effective way.

The Digital Sales Funnel

The digital sales funnel is a fundamental tool for any business that wants to succeed in the online world. It is a process that guides the customer from the moment they discover your product or service, until they finally make a purchase. The concept of a "funnel" is used because, just like in a real funnel, you start with many people at the top, and as they move through the different stages of the sales process, only some of them will reach the end and make a purchase. This process has several stages, and understanding each of them is key to creating a successful sales strategy.

The first stage of the digital sales funnel is "awareness." In this phase, the goal is to get the word out about your product or service. This is where potential customers encounter your brand for the first time. This can happen through various channels, such as social media ads, blog posts, YouTube videos, or even recommendations from other users. The important thing at this stage is to capture your audience's attention. To do this, it's essential that your message is clear, engaging, and resonates with the customer's needs or wants. Remember that at this stage, the customer isn't necessarily looking for a specific solution, but they may be interested in learning more about what you offer.

After the awareness stage, customers who are interested in what you offer will move on to the next stage of the funnel: the "consideration" stage. At this point, the customer has shown interest in your product or service and is looking for more information to decide if it is really what they need. This is where content plays a crucial role. In-depth articles, comparison guides, product reviews, demos, and testimonials can help the customer evaluate whether your offering is right for them. The goal at this stage is to nurture the customer with valuable information that helps them make an informed decision. You need to position yourself as an authority in your industry and demonstrate how your product or service can solve their problems or improve their life.

The third stage of the funnel is the "decision" stage. At this stage, the customer is ready to take a concrete action, but may still be considering different options. This is where you need to present an attractive offer that motivates them to choose your product over the competition. Promotions, special discounts, free shipping, or money-back guarantees are some of the tactics you can use to convince the customer to take the final step. At this point, it is essential to make the purchasing process as simple and smooth as possible. If the customer faces obstacles such as long forms, difficulties in paying, or lack of clear information, they are likely to abandon the process. That is why the user experience must be impeccable to facilitate conversion.

The final stage of the digital sales funnel is the "action" stage, where the customer finally makes the purchase. Although this is the main goal of the funnel, it doesn't mean that the process ends here. In fact, the relationship with the customer is just beginning. Once the customer has purchased, it's important to continue offering value to foster long-term loyalty. Sending follow-up emails, offering technical support, asking for reviews, and providing additional content on how to use the product are some of the ways you can maintain a positive relationship with the customer after the sale. A satisfied customer will not only buy again, but may also recommend your product to others, expanding your reach without you having to invest as much in acquiring new customers.

In addition to understanding the stages of the funnel, it is important to mention that each customer goes through this process at their own pace. Some customers may take weeks or even months to move from one stage to another, while others may make decisions quickly. The key to managing the digital sales funnel is to maintain constant and adequate communication at each stage of the process. It is not just about selling, but about creating a relationship with the customer that allows them to feel safe and supported at every step.

One cool aspect of the digital sales funnel is that you can measure every step of the process. With digital tools, you can know exactly how many people have seen your ad, how many have clicked on it, how many have visited your website, how many have added a product to their shopping cart, and how many have completed the purchase. This ability to track and analyze data gives you a huge advantage in optimizing your sales strategy. If you notice that many people are dropping out of the process at a specific stage, you can adjust your messaging or improve the user experience at that part of the funnel. This constant optimization will help you increase conversions and improve your business's bottom line.

Automation also plays a key role in the digital sales funnel. You can automate many aspects of the process so that customers receive the right message at the right time. For example, you can set up automated emails that are sent when a potential customer signs up to your site or shows interest in a specific product. These emails can offer more information, answer frequently asked questions, or even offer personalized discounts to incentivize the purchase. Automation not only saves time, but also ensures that customers don't get stuck at any stage of the funnel, moving more seamlessly towards the final purchase.

The digital sales funnel also allows for great segmentation. Not all customers are the same, and each may have different motivations and needs. With a well-designed funnel, you can create different messages and personalized offers for different segments of your audience. For example, a customer who has visited your website several times but has not yet purchased may receive an email with a special offer. While a customer who has previously purchased may receive recommendations for complementary products or information about new products that may interest them. This ability to personalize is one of the biggest benefits of the digital sales funnel, as it allows you to adapt to the specific needs of each customer.

Another advantage of the digital funnel is that it allows you to scale your sales efforts more efficiently. While in traditional sales, a salesperson can only serve one customer at a time, the digital funnel can work with thousands of potential customers simultaneously. By having an automated and well-structured process, you can reach a much wider audience without needing to proportionally increase your sales team. Not only does this save costs, but it also allows businesses to grow faster and more sustainably.

In short, the digital sales funnel is a powerful strategy that allows you to effectively attract, educate, and convert customers in the online environment. Understanding each of the stages of the funnel and how to optimize each step of the process is key to improving your conversion rates and increasing your sales. In addition, automation and personalization allow the funnel to work efficiently, without losing the human touch necessary to build long-lasting relationships with customers. By implementing a well-designed sales funnel, you will be better prepared to compete in the digital world and take your business to the next level.

Content Marketing

Content marketing is one of the most effective and powerful strategies in the world of sales and digital marketing. In essence, it is about creating and sharing valuable, relevant and consistent content to attract and retain a clearly defined audience, with the ultimate goal of motivating them to take a desired action, such as making a purchase or hiring a service. Unlike traditional advertising, which focuses on selling directly, content marketing seeks to offer useful and entertaining information that provides value to the customer, helping them solve problems or learn something new.

A key aspect of content marketing is that it's not just about talking about your product or service in a direct way. Instead, it's about building a relationship with your audience by providing them with content that they're genuinely interested in and that serves them in their everyday lives. This content can take many forms: blog posts, videos, infographics, podcasts, emails, social media posts, and more. The important thing is that the content is designed to address the needs, concerns, and desires of your target audience.

The reason content marketing is so effective is that consumers today are more informed and empowered than ever before. Before purchasing any product or service, most people research online, look for reviews, compare options, and take their time to make a decision. This is where content marketing comes into play: by offering useful information, you can position yourself as an authority in your industry and gain customer trust, which will eventually lead them to choose your brand over the competition.

The first step in a content marketing strategy is to know your audience. Before creating any content, you need to understand who your potential customers are, what problems they face, what interests they have, and what kind of information they are looking for. This will allow you to create content that really speaks to them and resonates with them. There is no point in generating quality content if it is not targeted to the right people. For example, if you sell technology products, your customers are likely to be interested in guides on how to use technology to improve their daily lives or reviews of the latest innovations on the market. On the other hand, if your audience is parents, they may prefer content related to education or family well-being.

Once you know your audience well, the next step is to create content that speaks to their needs. This is where creativity comes into play. Content should not only be informative, it should also be entertaining and easy to consume. A common mistake in content marketing is to create texts or videos that are too technical or difficult to understand. The goal is to make content accessible to anyone while also offering value to them. It's like having a conversation with your customers: you should speak in their language, using examples and references that they can understand.

Another important aspect of content marketing is consistency. It's not about creating an article or a video once in a while, but doing it consistently. Publishing content regularly not only keeps you top of mind with your customers, but it also helps improve your visibility on search engines like Google. Businesses that publish quality content on a frequent basis are much more likely to appear in the top search results, which increases their exposure and drives more traffic to their websites. That's why it's a good idea to create a content calendar that allows you to plan what you're going to publish and when. This way, you'll always have fresh and relevant content for your audience.

One of the great things about content marketing is that you can use it across different platforms to reach a wider audience. For example, you can write a blog post and then share snippets of it on social media like Facebook, Instagram, or LinkedIn to attract more people to your website. You can also turn that post into an explanatory video or an engaging infographic, allowing you to reach those who prefer to consume content visually. The key is to adapt your message to the format and platform, without losing sight of the main objective: providing value to your audience.

Content marketing is not only effective for attracting new customers, but also for retaining current ones. After someone has purchased your product or service, you can continue to offer them useful content to improve their experience or to show them new ways to use what they've purchased. For example, if you sell software, you could create tutorials that teach users how to get the most out of it, or send them regular updates about new features. This type of content not only increases customer satisfaction, but it also fosters long-term loyalty. A customer who feels that your company cares about them and continues to provide value is much more likely to make a repeat purchase or recommend your products to others.

Content marketing also has a direct impact on your brand image. By creating useful and relevant content, you are showing that your company is not just interested in selling, but in helping people solve their problems or improve their lives. This builds trust and positions you as a leader in your industry. Instead of being seen as a company that only seeks profit, you become a trusted source of information. And when people trust you, they are more likely to choose your brand when they need what you offer.

In addition to building trust, content marketing allows you to educate your potential customers. Sometimes, people don't buy a product simply because they don't fully understand how it can help them. By creating educational content, you can show them in a clear and detailed way how your product or service can solve their problems or meet their needs. For example, if you sell an innovative product that isn't widely known, you can write an article explaining how it works, what its benefits are, and why it's better than existing alternatives on the market. This type of content not only informs the customer, but also guides them towards a purchase in a natural way.

Another benefit of content marketing is that it's a long-term strategy. Unlike paid advertising, whose impact fades as soon as you stop investing money, the content you create can continue to generate results for months or even years. A good blog post or popular video can continue to attract traffic and generate sales long after it's been published. Plus, content can be repurposed and updated over time. An article you wrote a year ago can be revised and expanded with new information, giving it a new life without having to start from scratch.

In short, content marketing is a powerful tool that allows you to connect with your audience, build trust, educate your customers, and improve your online visibility. It is a strategy that, if executed correctly, can generate significant results in the long term. By focusing on creating valuable and relevant content for your audience, you will not only be attracting new customers, but also building strong relationships that will allow you to grow sustainably in the digital world.

The Power of Social Media in Mass Sales

The power of social media in mass sales is something that cannot be ignored in today's world. These platforms have become an essential tool for any business that wants to reach a wider audience and generate high sales volumes. Social media not only connects people around the world, but also provides an unprecedented opportunity for brands to directly interact with their potential customers, build relationships, and offer their products or services in a more intimate and human way.

One of the main advantages of social media is its massive reach. Millions, even billions of people, use platforms like Facebook, Instagram, TikTok, Twitter, and LinkedIn every day. This means that as a marketer, you have the ability to showcase your products to a global audience without the need for large upfront investments. With one post, one video, or even one comment, you can capture the attention of thousands of people at the same time. This ability to reach such a wide audience is something that was once only within reach of large corporations with huge advertising budgets. But today, any business, no matter its size, can have a significant presence on social media.

The power of social media also lies in the ease with which engaging content can be generated. Images, videos, stories, and reels are all visual tools that allow you to showcase products in a highly engaging way. Users are constantly interacting with this type of content, making it an ideal way to capture their attention. While quality of content is important, you don't need a cinematic production to be successful. Sometimes a simple image or a short, authentic video can create much more impact than a traditional advertisement. The key is to showcase the product in a way that is appealing to your audience and resonates with them on an emotional level.

Another reason why social media is so effective for mass sales is the power of recommendation. On these platforms, users have the possibility to easily share their opinions and experiences with their friends and followers. When someone buys a product and posts it on their social media, it's like they're advertising your brand for free. This type of recommendation has a huge impact, as people tend to trust what their friends or acquaintances tell them more than what they see in a paid ad. In addition, the opinions and reviews of other users play a fundamental role in making purchasing decisions, and social media makes it much easier to access this information.

The concept of virality is another crucial aspect of the power of social media. A piece of content that goes viral can bring a product or brand to millions of people in a matter of hours or days. There is no exact formula for making content go viral, but it generally comes down to creating something that is entertaining, exciting, or resonates deeply with your audience. When people find something they find interesting, they have a tendency to share it with their followers, and their followers in turn share it with their followers, creating a ripple effect. This kind of mass exposure is something that few other forms of marketing can achieve so quickly and without high costs.

Social media also allows for very precise targeting. Platforms like Facebook, Instagram, and LinkedIn collect a wealth of data about their users: their interests, location, age, gender, behaviors, and much more. As a marketer, you can leverage this information to target your ads or posts to a specific group of people who are more inclined to be interested in what you offer. Instead of spending money trying to reach everyone, you can focus your efforts on those who could actually become your customers. Not only does this increase the chances of generating sales, but it also reduces marketing costs, making your investment much more efficient.

Another great advantage of social media is direct interaction with customers. Through comments, direct messages, or even polls, you can get real-time feedback on what customers think of your products. This interaction allows you to quickly adjust your offering, improve customer service, and build stronger relationships with your audience. Customers like to feel heard, and social media offers a direct channel for brands to be in constant contact with them. Not only does this increase customer loyalty, but it can also improve your business' reputation.

Influencer marketing is another powerful strategy that has emerged thanks to social media. Influencers are people who have built a loyal audience on platforms like Instagram, YouTube, or TikTok, and who have the ability to influence the purchasing decisions of their followers. Collaborating with influencers can be a great way to reach a wider audience and generate massive sales, as these content creators often have an authentic connection with their audience. When an influencer recommends a product, their followers see it as a genuine recommendation, which increases the likelihood that they will trust the brand and make a purchase.

Additionally, social media allows you to measure the results of your efforts very precisely. The platforms offer analytics tools that allow you to see how many people have seen your posts, how many have interacted with them, and most importantly, how many have made a purchase as a direct result of your social media campaigns. This ability to measure return on investment (ROI) in real time is invaluable for marketers, as it allows you to adjust your strategies on the fly and ensure you are getting the best results possible.

One of the challenges businesses face when using social media to sell en masse is competition. Since these platforms are accessible to everyone, many companies are competing for the attention of the same audience. That's why it's important for your content to stand out. One way to do this is through authenticity. Social media users value transparency and honesty highly. It's not just about showing a perfect product, but about connecting with the audience in a genuine way, showcasing the brand's values and telling stories that are meaningful to them.

In short, social media has immense power to generate massive sales. Its reach, the possibility of going viral, precise segmentation, influencer marketing, and direct interaction with customers make it an indispensable tool for any business that wants to grow in the digital world. Leveraging these platforms in an intelligent and creative way can take your sales to levels that previously seemed impossible. However, it is important to remember that success on social media is not just about selling, but about building authentic relationships with your audience, offering value, and being present on a consistent basis. In this way, you will not only achieve massive sales, but you will also create a loyal customer base that will support you in the long term.

Becoming the Customer's Ally

Becoming a customer's ally is one of the most powerful strategies a salesperson can adopt to generate sustainable sales and build long-term relationships. Unlike a quick sale, where the only goal is to close the deal as quickly as possible, when you become a customer's ally, you are creating a connection of trust and collaboration that goes far beyond the initial transaction. Instead of focusing only on what you can gain, you focus on how you can help the customer solve their problems and achieve their goals. This not only benefits you in the short term, but opens the door to a long-lasting relationship where the customer will see you as someone they can trust, and this, in the long run, is what generates massive and sustainable sales.

The first step to becoming a customer's ally is to understand that sales isn't just about the product or service you're offering, but about the solution you're giving the customer. People aren't really interested in what you're selling, but how what you're selling can make their lives better or easier. Your job as a salesperson isn't just to describe the features of your product, but to deeply understand what the customer's needs and wants are, and then show them how your offering can meet those needs. If you position yourself as someone who is genuinely interested in helping, the customer will see you as a valuable resource, not just another salesperson.

To achieve this, it is essential to actively listen to the customer. This means paying attention to what they say, but also to what they don't say. Many times, customers don't know exactly what they need or how to express their problems clearly. This is where your role as an ally comes in: you must be able to read between the lines, ask the right questions, and guide the customer toward a solution they may not have considered. This type of approach shows that you really care about what the customer is looking for and that you are willing to put in the time and effort to find the best option for them.

Another important aspect of being a customer's ally is being honest and transparent at all times. It's not about selling at all costs. If a product or service you offer isn't what the customer needs, it's critical to let them know, even if it means losing a sale at that moment. This type of honesty may seem counterproductive in the short term, but it actually builds a relationship based on trust. Customers remember people who have been honest with them, and when they need something in the future, they'll come back to you because they know they can trust your judgment. Plus, they're very likely to recommend your business to others, simply because they appreciate your ethics and transparency.

Empathy is another key pillar to becoming a customer's ally. Putting yourself in the customer's shoes and understanding their situation from their perspective will allow you to offer much more personalized and effective solutions. It's not just about knowing what the customer needs on a superficial level, but understanding how they feel and what motivates them. If you can connect with the customer on an emotional level, you'll be able to offer value that goes beyond the material. This emotional connection is what differentiates an average salesperson from one who truly cares about their customers. People want to feel like they're more than just a number, and when they see that you take the time to understand their concerns and desires, a bond of loyalty is created that's hard to break.

Being a customer's ally also means being available to them, not just at the time of the sale, but afterward as well. Often, salespeople disappear once they've closed the deal, but that can be a big mistake. If you really want to become a customer's ally, you need to be there even after the transaction is over. This can mean following up to make sure everything is working properly, offering assistance, or simply being available to answer any questions that may arise. This type of after-sales care shows that your interest in the customer is not limited to the purchase, but that you care about their continued satisfaction.

Furthermore, being a customer's ally also means anticipating their needs. If you've built a solid relationship and taken the time to get to know your customer, you can begin to identify future opportunities where your products or services can be useful to them. This doesn't mean you should be pushy or aggressive in your offers, but you can be attentive to their changing situation or emerging needs. For example, if you know that a customer has purchased a technology product that tends to be updated frequently, you can anticipate their needs and offer them new versions or upgrades at the right time. This type of proactivity will be highly valued by the customer, as it shows that you care about their well-being and that you are thinking about their future.

Another way to be a customer's ally is to offer added value beyond what is expected. This can be something as simple as providing additional information to help them make more informed decisions or sharing useful resources that complement the product they've purchased. If, for example, you sell kitchen products, you could send recipes, cooking tips, or video tutorials that help the customer get the most out of their purchase. These types of gestures not only improve the customer experience, but also reinforce the idea that you care about their bottom line and not just the sale.

Being a customer's ally also means being flexible. Not all customers have the same needs or circumstances, and it's important that as a seller you can adapt to different situations. This can mean offering personalized options, being flexible with payment methods, or even adjusting delivery times based on the customer's needs. Flexibility shows that you're willing to do what it takes to make the shopping experience as convenient as possible for the customer, which in turn will strengthen the relationship you have with them.

Finally, it's important to remember that becoming a customer's ally isn't something that happens overnight. It's a process that takes time, patience, and dedication. It's about building genuine relationships based on trust, respect, and empathy. When you position yourself as an ally rather than just a salesperson, the customer will see you as someone who is on their side, someone they can trust and turn to when they need it. This type of relationship is what creates loyal and satisfied customers, and in the long run, that's what will lead to success in mass sales.

In short, becoming a customer's ally is one of the most effective ways to generate long-term sales and build a strong base of loyal customers. This is achieved through empathy, transparency, active listening, and a willingness to be present both before and after the sale. By focusing on the customer's needs and wants, and showing that you care about their success as much as your own, you position yourself as a valuable resource who not only sells products, but also provides meaningful solutions. Not only will this approach help you close more sales, but it will also allow you to build long-lasting relationships that are critical to sustained growth in the world of sales.

Customer Experience in the Digital Age

Customer experience in the digital age has completely transformed the way businesses interact with their consumers. In the past, the shopping experience was mostly limited to the physical world: visiting a store, speaking to a salesperson, reviewing products in person, and making a purchasing decision. Today, with the evolution of technology and the growing popularity of e-commerce, customers are interacting with brands in entirely new ways. The digital world has opened the door to a shopping experience that is faster, more convenient, and in many cases, more personalized. But it has also made customer expectations higher than ever.

In this digital age, customers are no longer just looking for a good product, they also expect an exceptional shopping experience. This includes smooth navigation on websites, fast and personalized support on chat platforms, fast and secure shipping, and the ability to access all the information they need instantly. Businesses that manage to offer this type of experience are the ones that stand out in the market and manage to generate a solid base of loyal customers.

One of the most important aspects of customer experience in the digital age is ease of use. Today's customers expect websites and apps to be intuitive and easy to navigate. If a customer enters an online store and finds it difficult to move between sections, add products to the cart or checkout, they will most likely leave the site and look for another option. Therefore, businesses need to ensure that their digital presence is as user-friendly as possible. Simplicity in design and ease of completing a purchase are key factors in keeping the customer engaged and satisfied.

Personalization is another crucial element of customer experience in the digital age. Businesses now have access to vast amounts of data about their customers – from what they search for to what they buy, and even how much time they spend browsing different products. This information allows brands to offer a much more personalized experience. Instead of displaying a generic catalog, they can suggest products that align with each customer's specific interests, making the shopping experience more relevant and engaging. Personalization can make the difference between a simple website visit and a concrete sale. When the customer feels that the brand understands them and offers them what they really need, they are much more likely to make a purchase.

Customer service in the digital age has also evolved greatly. Previously, if you had a question or problem with a product, you would have to call the company or visit them in person. Now, customer service is available 24/7 through different channels such as live chat, social media, email, and chatbots. This constant availability is a huge advantage for customers, who can now have their queries or problems resolved quickly and efficiently, no matter what time or place they are in. Companies that offer fast and effective customer service online are perceived as more trustworthy and accessible, which contributes to a positive shopping experience.

In the digital age, transparency has also become more important than ever. Customers want to know exactly what they are buying, how much it will cost, when they will receive their order, and what warranties they have. Thanks to technology, it is easier for companies to provide this information in a clear and detailed manner. Websites should include accurate product descriptions, high-quality images, reviews from other customers, and clear return policies. All of this information helps to build trust and improve the shopping experience. Plus, in a world where social media allows any bad experience to go viral in a matter of minutes, being transparent and resolving issues quickly is essential to protecting a brand's reputation.

Speed is another critical factor in customer experience in the digital age. Today's consumers expect everything to happen almost instantly. They are no longer willing to wait days for a response or weeks for a product to arrive. That's why businesses need to make sure their processes are as streamlined as possible, from customer service to shipping and delivering products. Platforms like Amazon have set a very high standard for speed of delivery, and customers now expect that same level of service everywhere. Businesses that can't meet these expectations risk losing customers to faster, more efficient competitors.

Another relevant aspect of customer experience in the digital age is the ability to offer multiple purchasing and payment options. Customers want to be able to choose how and when they buy. This means that businesses need to be present across different channels: online stores, mobile apps, social media, and more. Additionally, it is essential to offer various forms of payment, such as credit cards, bank transfers, mobile payments, and online payment services like PayPal. The more options the customer has, the more convenient the shopping experience will be, increasing the likelihood that they will complete their purchase and return in the future.

Social media also plays a pivotal role in customer experience in the digital age. Not only do these platforms allow brands to promote their products and services, but they also serve as a space where customers can interact directly with businesses. Whether through comments, direct messages, or reviews, social media provides a unique opportunity for brands to listen to their customers and respond to their needs quickly and publicly. Additionally, social media allows customers to share their experiences, whether positive or negative, which can influence the purchasing decisions of other consumers. Businesses that effectively use social media to engage with their customers and resolve issues quickly manage to significantly improve customer experience.

Trust and security are also key factors in customer experience in the digital age. With so many transactions happening online, customers want to be assured that their personal and financial data is protected. Businesses should invest in technologies that ensure the security of their customers' information, such as data encryption and secure payment systems. Additionally, it is important to be transparent about privacy policies and how customer data will be handled. Providing a safe and trustworthy shopping experience not only protects the customer, but also builds a strong reputation and improves long-term loyalty.

Finally, it is important to mention that the customer experience in the digital age does not end once the purchase has been made. Post-sale follow-up is essential to ensure that the customer is satisfied and to encourage future purchases. Companies must ensure that the customer receives their product on time, in good condition, and that they have access to assistance in case of any inconvenience. In addition, sending satisfaction surveys or offering discounts for future purchases can help keep the customer engaged and happy. This type of after-sale care not only improves the customer experience, but also increases the likelihood that that customer will recommend the brand to others.

In short, customer experience in the digital age is an essential aspect for the success of any business. In a world where competition is just a click away, offering a fast, convenient, personalized and secure shopping experience can be the difference between winning and losing customers. Companies that manage to adapt to the expectations of digital consumers and provide exceptional service, from the first click to post-sale follow-up, are the ones that manage to build long-term relationships and ensure their success in an increasingly competitive market.

Multichannel Sales

Multi-channel sales are a key strategy in today's world, where consumers interact with brands across multiple platforms and devices. It is no longer enough to sell only in a physical store or through a website. Today's customers expect the option to purchase in the way that is most convenient for them, whether in a physical store, online, through social media, or even through mobile apps. A multi-channel sales strategy allows businesses to reach customers across all of these touchpoints, offering an integrated and consistent shopping experience.

The main advantage of multi-channel sales is that it adapts to customer preferences. Some consumers prefer the convenience of shopping from home through a website, while others value the experience of visiting a physical store where they can see and touch the product before making a purchase decision. Others may feel more comfortable buying directly from social media channels like Instagram or Facebook, where brands promote their products in a more interactive way. With a multi-channel sales strategy, a company can capture the attention of all these types of customers, without missing any sales opportunities.

A key component of a multi-channel sales strategy is integrating all sales channels to deliver a unified experience. It's not just about being present on different platforms, but ensuring that the customer can move seamlessly between them. For example, a customer might see a product on a social network, read more details on the brand's website, and then decide to buy it in-store. The transition between these channels should be as natural as possible, without the customer feeling like they are starting from scratch on each platform. In fact, many consumers expect to be able to buy online and pick up their product in-store, or vice versa, return what they bought online to a physical store. These options are an example of how different channels can complement each other and offer a more satisfying experience for the customer.

Another benefit of multi-channel sales is that it allows brands to gain greater visibility. By being present on multiple platforms, companies can reach broader and more diversified audiences. A customer who doesn't frequent brick-and-mortar stores might find the brand online, while someone who isn't active on social media might discover the store while walking down the street. Each channel represents a new opportunity to attract different types of customers and strengthen the brand's presence in the market.

In addition, multi-channel selling also helps companies collect more data about their customers. Through different platforms, brands can learn more about their consumers' shopping habits: what they prefer, when they buy, how they discover new products, and more. This information is extremely valuable because it allows them to personalize the shopping experience and improve marketing strategies. For example, if a brand notices that many of its customers discover products on social media, it can focus more efforts on this channel, offering attractive content and exclusive promotions to capture attention. Similarly, if it notices that a large number of customers prefer to buy online but pick up in-store, it can optimize its logistics processes to make it more efficient.

However, implementing a multi-channel sales strategy also presents some challenges. The first is coordination between the different channels to ensure a consistent experience. This requires companies to maintain constant communication between the teams that manage each platform. In addition, it is important that information about products, prices and promotions is always up to date across all channels, to avoid confusion and potential customer dissatisfaction. If a customer sees one price online and then finds a different price in the physical store, this can lead to distrust and loss of the sale.

Another challenge is inventory management. With a multi-channel sales strategy, companies must ensure that inventory is synchronized across all channels. If a customer purchases a product online that is actually out of stock in the physical store, this can cause delays and frustration. Technology plays a key role in solving this problem, as it allows companies to manage their inventory in real time and ensure that products are available where and when the customer wants them.

In addition to operational challenges, multichannel selling requires significant investment in technology and staff training. Companies must have tools that allow them to manage the different platforms efficiently, as well as trained employees to serve customers on each channel. For example, physical store staff must be prepared to handle returns of products purchased online, and the customer service team must be trained to resolve issues both in physical stores and on digital platforms. All of this requires careful planning and a customer-centric approach.

Despite the challenges, the potential of multichannel sales is immense. Companies that manage to implement a well-executed multichannel strategy can not only increase their sales, but also improve customer satisfaction and strengthen long-term loyalty. By offering consumers the freedom to choose how and where they shop, brands position themselves as more flexible and focused on the needs of their customers, which generates greater connection and trust.

The future of sales is clearly heading towards a multi-channel approach. As consumers become more demanding and technologies continue to evolve, companies that fail to adapt to this new reality risk being left behind. Today's consumers are looking for convenience, personalization and accessibility, and multi-channel selling is the answer to these demands. Companies that are able to integrate all of their sales channels coherently and effectively will be better positioned to satisfy their customers and thrive in an increasingly competitive market.

In short, multichannel selling is more than just a trend, it's a necessity in today's business environment. Consumers are constantly moving between the digital and physical worlds, and brands must be prepared to meet them every step of the way. While it presents challenges, the benefits of a well-executed multichannel strategy are clear: increased visibility, more sales opportunities, an improved customer experience, and ultimately, a stronger, future-proof business.

Exponential Growth

Exponential sales growth is a concept that many companies dream of achieving, but few fully understand. It is growth that does not occur in a linear fashion, meaning it does not increase steadily and predictably. Instead, exponential growth follows a curve that shoots upward, doubling or multiplying results in a short period of time. This type of growth may seem surprising or even magical, but in reality, it is the result of a series of well-executed strategies, with a focus on innovation, efficiency and the smart use of resources.

To understand exponential growth, it's important to compare it to linear growth. If a company is growing linearly, it means that it's increasing its sales at a steady rate—say, 10 more units each month. In one year, it will have sold 120 more units than the year before. While this is positive, it's not surprising or groundbreaking. Exponential growth, on the other hand, might mean that instead of selling 10 more units per month, the company sells 10 more units in the first month, but 20 more in the second, 40 in the third, and so on. After one year, sales will have grown not by 120 units, but by thousands or more.

One of the keys to achieving this type of growth is understanding that it's not just about working harder, but working smarter. Companies that experience exponential growth have found ways to multiply their efforts through the use of technology, effective marketing strategies, and a deep understanding of their target audience. For example, many of these companies use the power of automation to streamline processes that would normally take a lot of time and effort. This frees up resources that can be invested in activities that truly generate value, such as product innovation or expansion into new markets.

Another crucial strategy for exponential growth is scalability. This means that the company must have the ability to increase its production or services without costs skyrocketing in the same proportion. A good example of this is the use of digital platforms. Before, a company that wanted to sell more products needed to open more physical stores, which involved a huge investment in infrastructure and staff. Today, thanks to online commerce, a company can reach millions of people around the world without needing to open a single additional store. This allows sales to grow rapidly without a proportional increase in costs.

Exponential growth also requires an open mindset toward innovation and change. Companies that cling to old methods of doing business often get stuck in linear growth. However, companies that are willing to try new ideas and adopt the latest technologies are the most likely to experience explosive growth. This may mean implementing new automation tools, exploring new sales channels like social media, or even adopting new ways of interacting with customers, such as using artificial intelligence to personalize the shopping experience.

One of the biggest contributors to exponential growth is virality. This is a concept that has been popularized with the rise of social media and digital platforms. When something goes viral, whether it's a product, a service, or an idea, it begins to spread rapidly from person to person, creating a chain effect. Imagine selling a product that not only solves a problem for the customer, but is also so unique and eye-catching that the customer feels the need to tell their friends, who in turn do the same. In no time, you have thousands or even millions of people interested in your product, without having to invest huge amounts in advertising. Virality is a powerful tool for exponential growth because it allows the market to work for you, multiplying your efforts almost automatically.

Another important feature of exponential growth is the ability to build a loyal community around your brand. Customers don't just buy a product, they feel like they're part of something bigger. This type of emotional connection can build long-term loyalty that not only keeps customers coming back again and again, but also turns them into advocates for your brand. This loyalty is what fuels exponential growth over time, as happy customers are the best ambassadors for your business. They talk about your product, recommend it, and most importantly, buy it again and again.

The use of advanced technology is also critical to this type of growth. Artificial intelligence, for example, allows businesses to collect and analyze vast amounts of data about their customers, helping them better understand their needs and behaviors. With this information, businesses can personalize their marketing offers and campaigns, increasing the chances of converting prospects into customers. Additionally, AI can automate repetitive tasks like customer service or inventory management, allowing the business to operate more efficiently and focus on strategies that truly drive growth.

However, exponential growth doesn't happen overnight. It requires planning, effort, and, above all, patience. A company must be willing to invest time in building a solid foundation before exponential growth really begins to take off. This may mean investing in technology, training the sales team, or simply making sure that products or services are of the highest quality. At first, the results may not be spectacular, but once a tipping point is reached, growth can accelerate at an impressive rate.

Finally, it's important to remember that exponential growth must be sustainable. Growing too quickly without the right infrastructure can cause more problems than it solves. Businesses need to ensure that their supply chain, customer service, and technology systems are prepared to handle the increase in demand. Otherwise, they risk disappointing customers and losing their hard-earned trust.

In short, exponential growth is the result of a combination of factors: scalability, innovation, technology, virality, and a community of loyal customers. It's not easy to achieve, but with the right strategy and an open mindset toward change, any company has the potential to achieve explosive growth. The most important thing is to always be willing to adapt, learn, and improve, because in the world of sales, success comes to those who are prepared to seize opportunities when they present themselves.

www.ingramcontent.com/pod-product-compliance
Lightning Source LLC
Chambersburg PA
CBHW031431150726
47989CB00002B/891